KV-371-232

This book is to be returned on or before
the last date stamped below.

Schools

ANCIENT EGYPT

Raintree

ANDREW LANGLEY

www.raintreepublishers.co.uk
Visit our website to find out more information about **Raintree** books.

To order:
 ☎ Phone 44 (0) 1865 888112
📄 Send a fax to 44 (0) 1865 314091
💻 Visit the Raintree Bookshop at **www.raintreepublishers.co.uk** to browse our catalogue and order online.

 Produced for Raintree by
White-Thomson Publishing Ltd
Bridgewater Business Centre, 210 High Street,
Lewes, East Sussex, BN7 2NH.

First published in Great Britain by Raintree, Halley Court,
Jordan Hill, Oxford OX2 8EJ, part of Harcourt Education.
Raintree is a registered trademark of Harcourt Education Ltd.

Editorial: Catherine Burch and Diyan Leake
Consultant: Dr Sharon McDermott
Design: Richard Parker
Page make-up: Mind's Eye Design Ltd, Lewes
Map artwork: Martin Darlison, Encompass Graphics
Picture Research: Elaine Fuoco-Lang
Production: Amanda Meaden
Originated by Dot Gradations
Printed and bound in Hong Kong, China
by South China Printing Company

ISBN 1 844 43361 7
09 08 07 06 05
10 9 8 7 6 5 4 3 2 1

British Library Cataloguing in Publication Data
Langley, Andrew
History in Art: Ancient Egypt
709.3'2
A full catalogue record for this book is available from the
British Library.

Acknowledgements

The publishers would like to thank the following for permission to
reproduce photographs (t = top, b = bottom, l = left, r = right): The
Art Archive/Dagli Orti pp. **9**(r) (Egyptian Museum Cairo), **12**
(Musee du Louvre Paris), **15** (Pharaonic Village Cairo), **16, 19, 22,
23**(t) (Pharaonic Village Cairo), **23**(b), **28**(b), **28**(t) (Musee du
Louvre, Paris), **29** (British Museum), **31**(t), **33**(bl) (Eileen Tweedy),
36 (British Museum/Jacqueline Hyde), **39**(t), **41**(b) (Egyptian
Museum Cairo), **43**(r); Bridgeman Art Library pp. **24** (The Stapleton
Collection), **25**(r) (Giraudon); Getty Images/PhotoDisc pp. **1, 4, 5,
45**; Dr Sharon McDermott p. **33**(br); Robert Partridge: The Ancient
Egypt Picture Library pp. **3, 6, 7**(t&b), **8, 9**(l), **10, 11**(t&b), **13**(t&b),
14, 17, 18, 20, 21(t&b), **25**(l), **26, 27**(t&b), **30, 31**(b), **32, 33**(t), **34,
35, 37, 38, 39**(b), **40, 41**(t), **42, 43**(l), **44**.

Cover photograph of a statue of Tutankhamen reproduced with
permission of the Art Archive.

Every effort has been made to contact copyright holders of any
material reproduced in this book. Any omissions will be rectified
in subsequent printings if notice is given to the publishers.

The publishers would like to thank Robert Partridge for his
assistance with captions and annotations.

Disclaimer

All the Internet addresses (URLs) given in this book were valid at
the time of going to press. However, due to the dynamic nature of
the Internet, some addresses may have changed, or sites may have
changed or ceased to exist since publication. While the author, the
packager and publishers regret any inconvenience this may cause
readers, no responsibility for any such changes can be accepted by
either the author, the packager or the publishers.

The paper used to print this book comes from sustainable resources.

Contents

Chapter 1   The art of ancient Egypt   4

Art as evidence   6

Chapter 2   The story of ancient Egypt   8

The Old Kingdom   10

The Middle Kingdom   12

The New Kingdom   14

Chapter 3   Land of the pharaohs   16

Building the pyramids   18

Trade and empire   20

Valley of the Kings   22

Greeks and Romans   24

Chapter 4   Everyday life   26

Eating and drinking   28

At work   30

Entertainment   32

Scribes and hieroglyphs   34

Chapter 5   Religion and mythology   36

Mummification   38

Burial   40

Priests and rituals   42

Timeline   44

Glossary   46

Further resources   47

Index   48

Words included in the glossary are in **bold** the first time they appear in each chapter.

The art of ancient Egypt

About 5000 years ago, a great empire grew up on the banks of the River Nile in Egypt. It was to last for more than 3000 years, far longer than any other **civilization** in history. During this vast period of time the Egyptians built some of the most gigantic and magnificent structures ever seen, including the great pyramids at Giza. This group was celebrated as one of the **Seven Wonders of the World**, and is the only one still standing today. An astonishing variety of temples, statues, carved stonework, wall paintings and jewellery have also survived.

Rediscovery

Nobody knew about these astonishing works for a long time. Much of the art of the ancient Egyptians lay buried or forgotten for many centuries after their empire came to an end. The meaning of their beautiful **hieroglyphic** texts (using signs and pictures) was lost. Treasures were robbed from the tombs, and stone blocks from the pyramids were taken to build other monuments.

It was only in the late 18th century that people began to take a serious interest in this lost civilization. In 1798 the French Emperor Napoleon marched into Upper Egypt with his armies and a group of scholars, who made a detailed record of the land and its monuments. This was the beginning of **Egyptology**. The pillaging of tombs and temples was stopped, sites were carefully excavated, and museums opened to house the findings.

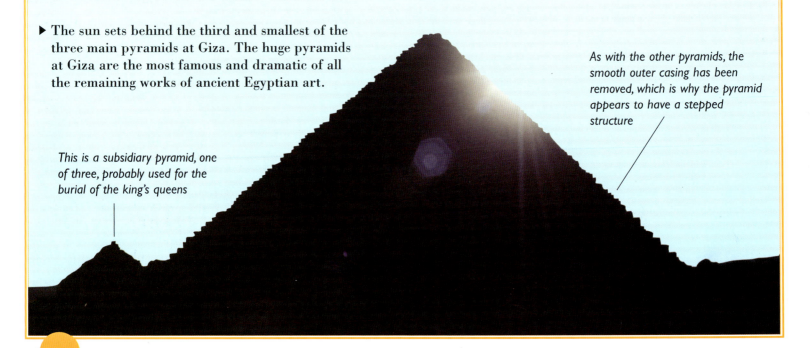

▶ The sun sets behind the third and smallest of the three main pyramids at Giza. The huge pyramids at Giza are the most famous and dramatic of all the remaining works of ancient Egyptian art.

As with the other pyramids, the smooth outer casing has been removed, which is why the pyramid appears to have a stepped structure

This is a subsidiary pyramid, one of three, probably used for the burial of the king's queens

Egyptian influence

The rediscovery of these long-lost works had a huge impact on all forms of art. The subject appeared in fiction and poetry, from Shelley's famous short poem 'Ozymandias' of 1819 to William Golding's story *The Scorpion God* of 1971. Many plays and films took their inspiration from ancient Egypt (at least six films have been made about the Egyptian Queen Cleopatra alone). Artists from Piranesi to Picasso were influenced by the techniques of the Egyptians.

Egyptian art had an even greater effect on architecture and design. From the 18th century Egyptian-style furniture and ornaments, such as **obelisks**, **sphinxes** and even mummy cases, adorned wealthy homes. The **Art Deco** style of the 1920s made use of formal Egyptian patterns and shapes for interior design. The Egyptian pyramid has been copied countless times by architects, for everything ranging from a casino in Las Vegas to the glass entrance to the Louvre in Paris.

▼ The major sites in ancient Egypt. They are all close to the River Nile, which flows through the middle of the land.

▼ The Great Sphinx at Giza crouches in front of the pyramid of Khafra, standing guard over the **pharaoh** inside. Completed in about 2500 BC, it was the first truly enormous sculpture in ancient Egypt – it is 73 metres long and 20 metres high.

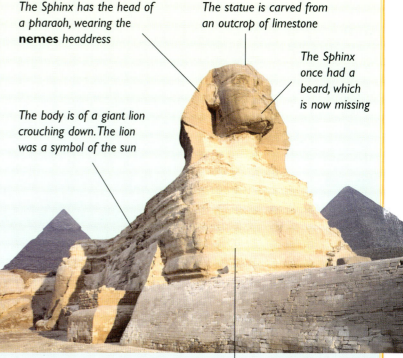

The Sphinx has the head of a pharaoh, wearing the **nemes** *headdress*

The statue is carved from an outcrop of limestone

The Sphinx once had a beard, which is now missing

The body is of a giant lion crouching down. The lion was a symbol of the sun

You can clearly see the different strata (layers) of stone. Some are softer and have worn away more quickly

Map

Mediterranean Sea

SYRIA

PALESTINE

Alexandria

N
W   E
S

Giza
Saqqara

LOWER EGYPT

LIBYA

Beni Hasan
El-Amarna

Nile

Valley of the Kings
Deir el-Bahri   Karnak
Medinet Habu   Thebes

Red Sea

Aswan

UPPER EGYPT

Abu Simbel

| 0 | 100 | 200 miles |
| 0 | 100 | 200 km |

Historic sites in Egypt
- ● City
- ▲ Pyramid
- ◩ Temple
- ▯ Tomb

NUBIA

The Mummy

Egyptian mummies have fascinated the Western world for centuries. Medieval merchants sold mummy fragments in a supposedly magic potion. Mummies have often featured in films. The most famous of these are *The Mummy*, starring Boris Karloff (1932), and the much later film of the same name starring Brendan Fraser (1999).

Art as evidence

We can study the art treasures of ancient Egypt in many places. There are many sites in Egypt to visit, and closer to home there are museums which house Egyptian **artefacts**. Images of sculptures, paintings and other works can be seen in books and on websites. All of these are a rich source of evidence about how the Egyptians lived and worked and what they believed – as long as we study them closely and carefully.

▼ The *Book of the Dead*, created in about 1310 BC, is among the oldest illustrated text yet discovered. The **papyrus** pages contain prayers and magic spells written in hieroglyphics, and illustrations of episodes from the soul's journey in the afterlife.

Artists or craftsmen?

The first question to ask is: who made these things? Painters, carvers and goldsmiths were not seen as artists in ancient Egypt. They were simply craft workers, and their task was to create completely clear images of people and animals. Egyptians believed that these images would take the place of the people's bodies after they died, and preserve them for their afterlife, or life after death.

Almost all of the craftsmen's work was connected to religion, because religion was at the centre of ancient Egyptian life. So they were employed, supervised and paid by priests or by officials of the king. Carpenters, sculptors, jewellers and others worked together in art studios near the palace or where their creations were needed, such as the building site of a pyramid or temple.

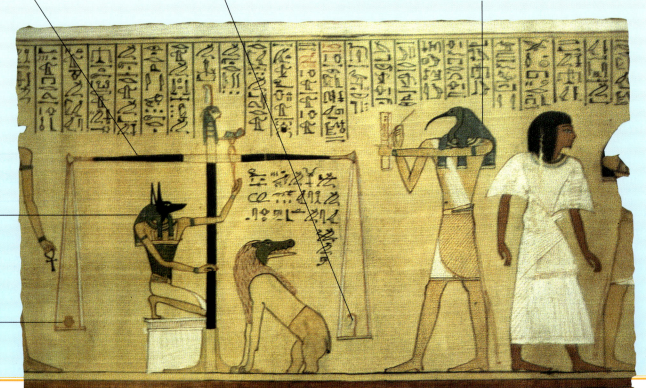

The scales of justice, used to weigh the dead person's heart against the feather of maat *(the symbol of truth)*

The feather of maat

Thoth, scribe of the gods, records the result. Thoth is usually given the head of an **ibis**, *with a long pointed bill*

The jackal-headed god Anubis, protector of the dead

The dead person's heart

What can art tell us?

Without the buildings, carvings and other art objects we would know very little about ancient Egypt. Such objects give vivid pictures of Egyptian life and death, from battle paintings to clay figures of men and women. If we examine the objects on different levels we can find out much more than is obvious at first glance. For example, we can look at the techniques of the craftsmen, the strict rules they had to work to, and the people they worked for.

One interesting aspect of a work of art to consider is where the materials came from to make the objects. Soft stone was brought from the Nile valley, harder stone came from the nearby desert. Good timber, gold and other precious things had to be imported from much further away – probably Lebanon or central Africa. Knowing what materials were used we can deduce something about Egyptian trade.

▼ This is a scene from the outside of the **hypostyle** hall of the temple at Karnak. Built for King Seti I, the wall is decorated with scenes of his military campaigns. This is probably part of his victory parade on his return to Egypt, as he looks back over lines of manacled prisoners. There is a line of prisoners in front of his chariot too, about to be paraded before the god of the temple, Amun.

▶ This painted relief carving showing King Tuthmose III (on the right) making offerings to the god Horus, is from the mortuary temple of Queen Hatshepsut at Deir el-Bahri. The king holds two jars in his hand. The god is shown with the head of a **falcon**.

The whole picture

The figures in ancient Egyptian paintings and **relief** carvings are painted quite differently from present-day styles and may look strange to us. This style, called frontalism, means that the head is always drawn in profile (turned to the side), while the body is seen from the front. Although the face is turned to the side, the eye is seen in full. The legs turn to the same side as the head. The artists wanted to illustrate the whole of a person's body, and not just a part of it seen from one angle. They believed that by depicting the whole body, they were preserving it for eternity.

He holds a sword in his hand

Protective vultures hover over his head, as does a winged sun disc

Harnesses decorated with ostrich feathers

Seti I about to get into his chariot

Chariot is pulled by two horses

The story of ancient Egypt

The first settlers came to Egypt about 15,000 years ago. They were probably cattle herders, who wandered across northern Africa in search of water and grazing for their animals. A large area of the country was green and hospitable, with good supplies of grass and low trees, and regular rainfall. The settlers learned to grow crops, and found plenty of game to hunt. Then, about 12,000 years ago, the climate is believed to have changed. The rainfall dwindled, the streams dried up and much of the region became desert.

The gift of the river

People were forced to move to the valley of the River Nile. This narrow strip of land hugging both sides of the river was still lush and fertile, thanks to the annual floods. Every July, the Nile was swollen by the rains that fell on hills and mountains far to the south. The river burst its banks and flooded the surrounding land, spreading a rich mud over the fields. By September the water was low enough for people to sow seeds, and the crops ripened so fast in the sun that they were ready to harvest in short and calculated periods of time.

Herodotus, the ancient Greek historian, described this natural miracle as the 'Gift of the Nile'. The early farmers were able to arrange their lives to fit in with the pattern of the flood. They could grow up to four different crops in a single year, one after the other. Besides this, the river gave them mud to make pots and bricks, as well as a supply of fish. Animals, such as gazelles and geese, were killed for meat.

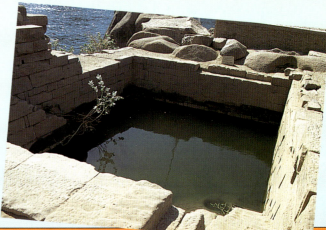

▼ This is a Nileometer on the island of Elephantine at Aswan, fed by a short canal from the River Nile. The purpose of Nileometers was to determine the level of the annual flood.

Nileometer

Ancient Egyptians measured the rise and fall of the River Nile. The Nile rose in Aswan which is in the south of the country. Knowing the level was important: too high and property could be damaged, too low and there was the prospect of a poor harvest. The information may have been used to determine the amount of the future harvest to be taken in taxes. The grand Nileometer on Elephantine Island at Aswan was a steep staircase, with 90 steps which ran down the side of the island into the water. As the floods rose, the water covered more steps. Priests from the nearby temple noted the changing level each day with a mark on the wall, and kept accurate records throughout the year. There were Nileometers all along the river, but only a few of the ancient ones have survived.

▶ The cliffs and valleys near the Nile were rich in many types of stone. One of the most useful of these was flint, which could be shaped into axes, spearheads and other tools and weapons. This elaborate flint-bladed knife is a superb example of the skills of the ancient flint workers. It is known as the Gebel el-Arak knife. The style of art on the handle does not appear to be Egyptian and it may be an imported piece. It dates from the very earliest years of the Egyptian **civilization**.

Ivory handle carved with small figures of men fighting and in boats

The blade is known as a 'ripple flaked' blade, because of its distinctive shape

Razor-sharp edge

The strokes used to work the flint to shape can be clearly seen

Egypt united

By about 5000 BC, small villages had grown up along the Nile. **Archaeologists** have found pottery from this period, along with fine carvings in **ivory** and stone. This shows that farming was so easy that not everyone was needed to work in the fields. Some people developed craft skills, while others began trading goods with other communities.

Districts grew up with their own identity, their own leaders and their own gods. These districts became bigger as they merged with, or conquered, one another until there were two main districts – Upper Egypt in the south, and Lower Egypt in the north. In around 3100 BC, these two were gradually amalgamated by King Menes of Upper Egypt.

▼ Carved slabs of slate have been discovered in several graves from this period. They are called palettes, and are some of the earliest pieces of Egyptian art to have survived. The most famous is the Narmer Palette, which shows the figure of a king. His name was Narmer, and he was probably the same person as Menes, the first unifier of Egypt.

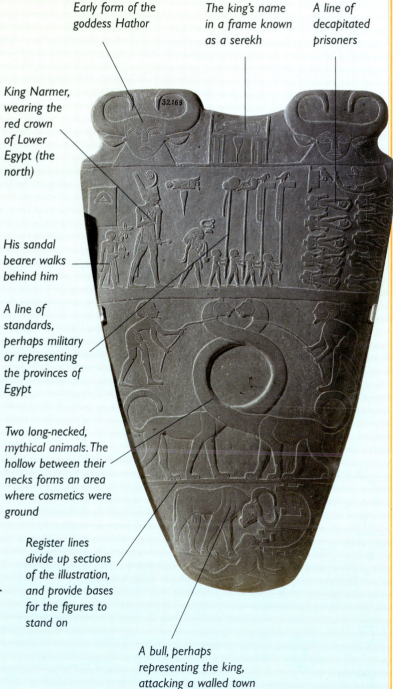

Early form of the goddess Hathor

The king's name in a frame known as a serekh

A line of decapitated prisoners

King Narmer, wearing the red crown of Lower Egypt (the north)

His sandal bearer walks behind him

A line of standards, perhaps military or representing the provinces of Egypt

Two long-necked, mythical animals. The hollow between their necks forms an area where cosmetics were ground

Register lines divide up sections of the illustration, and provide bases for the figures to stand on

A bull, perhaps representing the king, attacking a walled town

The Old Kingdom

Menes (or Narmer) was the first king of the First **Dynasty** of ancient Egypt. His people believed that he was descended from the gods, and so all the rulers who succeeded him must be gods as well. This gave the kings of Egypt total power over their subjects. Over the next 3000 years there were to be more than 150 kings and queens, grouped into over 30 dynasties or families. Historians have divided these dynasties into three major periods. The first, called the Old Kingdom, lasted from 2686 BC to about 2180 BC. This was the age of the pyramids.

▼ The Step Pyramid at Saqqara was built in *c.* 2700 BC. Imhotep, the architect, made the bold decision to use stone instead of the usual timber or mud-brick which soon rotted or washed away. The stone blocks are small compared with those in later pyramids.

Governing Egypt

The most famous legacy of the Old Kingdom is the pyramids. King Djoser, during the Third Dynasty, had the Step Pyramid built at Saqqara, and later kings built the three massive pyramids at Giza. The mere fact that these huge structures exist tells us a lot about early Egyptian society. It was obviously well organized, with a powerful ruler who could assemble a vast force to do the construction work.

The king's authority came from his status as a god, but the daily government of the country was done by ministers and officials. The most important of these was the **vizier**, or prime minister, who was responsible for everything from the law courts and tax collection to building projects and grain storage. Egypt was divided into *nomes* or districts, each governed by a local official called a *nomarch*.

The six huge steps of the pyramid symbolize the passing of the dead king's soul as it ascends towards the sun god

The pyramid rises to a height of 60 m

The pyramid was once clad in white limestone, but only the core blocks now survive

The burial chamber is beneath the pyramid

Prosperity and decline

Most of the pyramid workforce was made up of Egyptian agricultural workers and foreign prisoners. During the Fourth Dynasty, armies captured these prisoners during Egyptian invasions of Nubia and Libya. This period saw Egypt grow in power and wealth. The military expeditions brought control of important sources of minerals and luxury goods. Trade flourished, with Egyptian merchants buying gold, **ebony** and skins in exchange for linen, honey and oil.

Trouble was coming, however. By about 2180 BC many *nomarchs* had become independent, and they challenged the power of the king. **Civil war** broke out, and the unrest was made worse by famine. For a long and disastrous spell, the Nile did not rise to its normal flood levels and crops failed. There were riots, tombs were destroyed, and it is claimed that in parts of Upper Egypt there was **cannibalism**.

▼ These statues of Prince Rahotep and his wife Nofret are two of the best-preserved statues to have survived from ancient Egypt. They were found in the couple's tomb at Meidum. Both figures are slightly larger than life-size and retain almost all of their original paint.

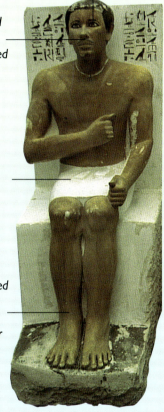

Both statues have remarkably life-like eyes made of rock crystal

Rahotep has short cropped hair and a neatly trimmed moustache

He wears a short white kilt

His skin is shown as a red ochre colour, the artistic convention for showing men

Nofret has a large heavy wig over her natural hair

Elaborate collar and diadem

She wears a tightly fitting white dress

Her skin is painted in yellow ochre, the colour always used for women

Mastabas

Archaeologists have found many massive mud-brick tombs called **mastabas**, both near the Step Pyramid at Saqqara and throughout the country. These were probably built to house the bodies of important officials. They were constructed over chambers cut into the solid rock and had several painted rooms which were once filled with treasures and beautifully made grave goods.

◄ This mastaba is one of hundreds of tombs at Saqqara grouped around the Old Kingdom pyramid tombs of the kings. The doors to this mastaba are modern. There would have been wooden doors in place when the tomb was new.

The Middle Kingdom

The Old Kingdom ended in civil war and chaos. Egypt went though a long period of instability until it was split up again into many small states with rulers who fought against each other. It was not until about 2061 BC that Mentuhotep II defeated all rivals and united the country again. A new era of peace began, known as the Middle Kingdom.

New rulers, new gods

Mentuhotep came from the city of Thebes in Upper Egypt, which became the new centre of power. He re-established control over the regions and appointed Theban officials to govern them. He and later kings took a firm hand with the *nomarchs*, demanding taxes and troops from them.

Religion changed too. The kings of the Old Kingdom had worshipped Re, the sun god, but the Theban rulers of the Twelfth Dynasty had their own local **deities**. They dedicated many temples to traditional gods such as Osiris and Thoth, and also promoted Amun, who they believed had created the world. Amun was unseen and mysterious, and so kings were able to alter the way artists depicted him to suit their political purposes. However, Re was to remain an important god for many centuries.

▼ The relationships between Egyptian gods and kings are complicated and confusing. This **papyrus**, part of the *Book of the Dead*, shows Re.

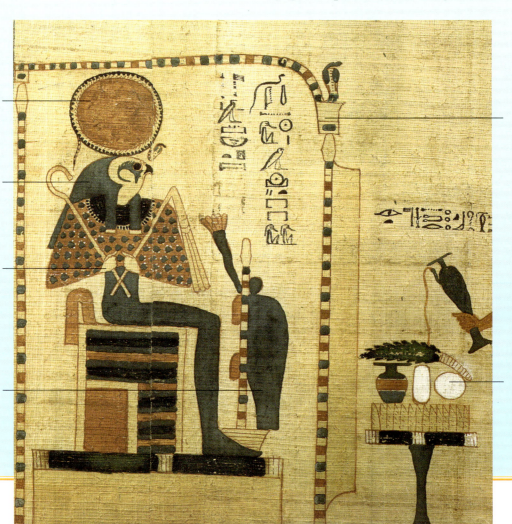

The sun's disc, surrounded by a cobra

Re, with the head of a hawk

A crook and a flail, symbols of royalty

This strange object is an inflated animal skin mounted on a pole, standing in a stone jar. It is the emblem of Osiris, the god of the dead

Poles support a canopy, to give Re shade, with doors which stand open

An offering table heaped with food, with someone pouring a libation (drink offering), probably of water, over it

▶ The hippopotamus was loved and feared by the Egyptians. They loved it as Taweret, the goddess of fertility and childbirth. They feared hippos as a danger to boats on the Nile and as destroyers of crops. This superb model dates from the Middle Kingdom.

Hippo is a comfortable round shape, suggesting the bulges of pregnancy

Body of the animal is decorated with drawings of river plants, probably referring to the regenerative effect of the river

Keeping control

Egypt grew calm and prosperous again. The kings protected the country's border against invaders by building a line of huge mud-brick fortresses along the southern part of the Nile in about 1860 BC, and another near the **delta** region in the north. Trading expeditions were sent to Syria and Palestine to obtain **incense** and other luxury goods.

The increase in wealth led royalty and other important families to build many grand new tombs and temples. Mentuhotep II's tomb at Deir el-Bahri occupied builders, architects, painters and sculptors for 25 years before it was completed. Another notable site was at Beni Hasan on the east bank of the Nile, where rock tombs were decorated with many superb paintings showing rare scenes from everyday and military life. Vast **granite** statues, such as the **sphinx** of King Ammenemes II, also show how rulers wanted to impress their gods with sheer size.

Hippo is made of a glazed material known as faience

The distinctive blue colour comes from copper

▼ The entrance to the Temple of Amun at Karnak. Originally the gateway would have been closed with great wooden doors. It is the first of six gateways, leading to the heart of the temple. In front and to either side of the pathway into the temple is an avenue of ram-headed sphinxes. The ram was the sacred animal of the god Amun.

Karnak

The Temple of Amun at Karnak, near Thebes, is one of the biggest religious complexes ever created. Begun in about 1990 BC, it was massively extended and rebuilt over the next five centuries.

The New Kingdom

By the time of the Thirteenth Dynasty, Egypt was once again split by civil war. Her rulers were weak, and by 1663 BC foreign invaders had swept into the Nile delta and taken charge. These were known as the Hyksos, or 'kings of foreign lands', and probably came from Asia. They brought stability and advanced military skills to the country, but were hated by Egyptians because they were invaders. The Hyksos were driven out in about 1570 BC by the Theban rulers Kamose and Ahmose.

Richer than ever

Ahmose became the first king of the Eighteenth Dynasty and the founder of what we call the New Kingdom. Over the next 500 years, ancient Egypt reached a new peak of power and wealth. The strongest rulers of the Eighteenth Dynasty pushed the frontier eastwards as far as the River Euphrates (in modern Iraq) and south into Nubia. Increased contact with other lands brought a flood of riches, which were used to build even more magnificent palaces, tombs and temples.

Among the strongest of the New Kingdom rulers was a woman, Hatshepsut. She was married to Tuthmose II and seized the throne when he died in 1498 BC. Hatshepsut reigned for 20 years, and left behind one of the finest of all works of Egyptian architecture, her mortuary temple at Deir el-Bahri.

▶ One of the most famous works of art from ancient Egypt is this limestone bust of Queen Nefertiti (wife of King Akhenaten), which dates from about 1344 BC. It was made as a 'master' image of the queen for other artists to use as a model. For this reason it is unusual, because there is no body. The Egyptians did not make portrait busts otherwise. The head was found, along with other sculptures, in the artist's studio at El-Amarna in Middle Egypt. The survival of the paint is unusual, and the image is considered to be a true likeness of the queen, much more realistic than royal portraits from other periods.

The tall, flat-topped crown is unique to her

The crown is circled by a diadem, at the front of which was an image of the royal cobra (which is now lost)

The sculpture was designed to stand on its own

The queen wears an elaborate collar

Akhenaten's revolution

Through their long history, the ancient Egyptians wanted stability and feared change. So the short reign of King Amenhotep IV (1367–1360 BC) came as a terrible shock. Amenhotep rejected the old gods, Re and Amun, and in their place worshipped Aten, the 'sun disc' and creator of all living things. He changed his name to Akhenaten (meaning 'agreeable to the Aten') and founded a new royal city (now called El-Amarna) far to the north of Thebes.

Akhenaten had made a bold break from the past. He suppressed the old gods and closed their temples. He encouraged a new and more realistic attitude in painters and sculptors, asking them to depict people in natural poses rather than the traditional idealized ones. Sadly, Akhenaten's revolutionary ideas were doomed to fail. The priests of Amun rebelled in fury at his measures, and after his early death there was a swift return to the old religion.

▶ This is a replica of the mummy of King Tutankhamen. The original is still in the tomb in Luxor. The body was originally enclosed in three coffins.

Finding Tutankhamen

When Akhenaten's son succeeded him, he was only nine years old. He took the name of Tutankhamen, in honour of the old god of Egypt. His reign was short, but today he is the most famous of all the Egyptian kings. His fame comes from the sensational rediscovery of his tomb by archaeologist Howard Carter in 1922 – sensational because it had lain almost untouched since he was buried. Nearly every other royal tomb had been stripped by robbers over the centuries, but Tutankhamen's still contained most of its amazing treasures, including the three gold coffins which held the king's mummified body. **Egyptologists** are still studying and learning from this extraordinary hoard.

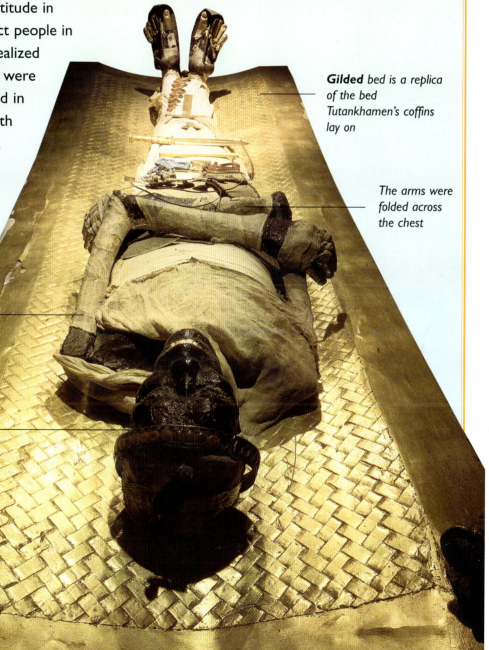

Gilded bed is a replica of the bed Tutankhamen's coffins lay on

The arms were folded across the chest

The young king's face, arms and legs have shrivelled up in the drying process

This broad band of gold held a linen skull-cap in place before the mummy was wrapped up

Bed is wooden, overlaid with gold

Land of the pharaohs

'His eyes probe every being … He illumines Egypt more brightly than the sun … He makes things greener than the great flood … He fills Egypt with strength and life … His enemies will be made poor.' These are some of the opening lines of a text from Middle Kingdom times, and they make it plain that the king was by far the most important and powerful person in the land. He was such a mighty figure that he was not referred to by his name or title, but simply as the **pharaoh**, meaning 'great house' or 'palace'.

A living god

The pharaoh was not just the most powerful person in Egypt and its leader in battle. He was also a god from the moment he was crowned, directly descended from Re or Amun. Tomb paintings often show the king being supported by two other gods – Horus, patron god of the pharaohs, and Seth, god of storms, violence and warfare.

The king or queen had absolute power over their subjects, but they also had many duties. They were thought to be able to communicate with other gods and to provide divine guidance and protection to the people. The king appeared before the people in a series of ceremonies throughout the year.

▼ Horemheb became king in about 1320 BC. He had a new tomb constructed in the Valley of the Kings, where this painting was found.

Ceremonial costume of **nemes** headdress and false beard to show authority

These oval shapes containing the names and titles of kings are known as cartouches

The red and white crowns of Upper Egypt (the south)

The **falcon** head of the god Horus

The god Horus welcomes the king

Horus holds an ankh, the symbol used to denote eternal life

Some ceremonies were connected with founding new temples, others with the annual flooding of the Nile. A special ceremony took place when a king had reigned for 30 years. This was not just a celebration of his jubilee, but also a test to demonstrate that he was still healthy and strong. Some **relief** carvings depict this test, in which the king had to run round a track or palace yard.

Wives and children

Kings usually had several wives, but from the New Kingdom period only one was given the titles 'Great Royal Wife' and 'Lady of the Two Lands'. She would often be a close relative (though only rarely a sister), so that the purity of the royal bloodline was maintained, and to prevent jealousy from rival families. The chief wife's children would be next in line for the throne.

▶ This is a wooden *ushabti* figure from the tomb of Tutankhamen. *Ushabtis* were 'worker figures', or servants who could be called on in the afterlife. Tutankhamen had several hundred buried with him in his tomb. The figures range from a few centimetres in height to around half a metre. This is one of the larger and better examples.

Portrait of a pharaoh

The kings and queens of ancient Egypt live on today in the paintings and carvings of them. They are almost always shown in ceremonial costume, with the symbols of their divine power. The *ushabti* figure below from Tutankhamen's tomb resembles coffin and mask 'portraits' of the young king.

Headdress diadem in the shape of a cobra, one of the symbolic creatures which protected kings

The nemes, a striped headdress which hangs down on both sides of the face

The figure is made of wood, with details painted on

A crook, symbol of leadership and government

A flail (another symbol of power)

17

Building the pyramids

The pharaoh may have been a god, but he knew that one day he was going to die. So, as soon as he became king, he began to prepare for his death by planning and building a suitably grand tomb. During the Old Kingdom period, royal tombs grew more massive and elaborate, starting with the mud-brick **mastabas** and reaching their climax in the vast pyramids that were built by successive kings at Giza around 2600 BC.

▼ View of the Great Pyramid of Khufu at Giza, seen from the north. This is the largest pyramid ever built in Egypt. The stones were once covered with fine white limestone blocks, but these were looted many years ago. A few blocks can be seen in the middle of the base.

The Great Pyramid

The giant among these structures was the Great Pyramid of Khufu, who came to the throne in about 2550 BC. His pyramid is an astonishing achievement of engineering and design. The base is almost exactly level, and the corners are almost exact right angles. Each of the four sides is about 230 metres long (and they vary by no more than 4.4 centimetres), and the pyramid rises to a height of more than 146 metres. It contains about 2,300,000 blocks of stone, weighing an average of 2.5 tonnes each.

The Great Pyramid was probably planned by the king, his **vizier** and his chief architect. There were two good reasons for them to choose the site at Giza.

Workers laid the casing (outer) stones over the core (inner) layers. A kind of cement was used to fill gaps between the blocks to bind them together

The original entrance to the pyramid. Visitors now enter the pyramid through a smaller entrance, cut by tomb robbers, to the right of the original entrance

A few white limestone blocks remain

The blocks of stone get smaller as they rise from the base to the top

First, the flat land was strong enough to stand the enormous weight of the stone; and, second, it was near enough to a harbour on the Nile for the materials to be transported by river and landed close by. The architect then began to design the structure and work out how much stone would be needed.

Muscle power

First the outline of the pyramid was marked out. Khufu led a special religious **ritual**, in which he drove stakes into the four corners of the site and laid the first stone. After this, the builders set to work. The project must have taken at least 23 years to complete, which means that more than 300 stone blocks had to be laid every day (one every two minutes). Historians estimate that a regular workforce of at least 25,000 men was needed to do this.

The builders had no cranes, pulleys or scaffolding, and no mechanical tools. They had to work with simple implements, including stone hammers, copper saws and chisels, and wooden **squares**. With these they cut and shaped very hard stone, such as **granite** and **basalt**, as well as the softer limestone.

The blocks came by boat from quarries near the Nile, and were hauled to the site on sleds along tracks made slippery with water, milk or oil. As the pyramid rose higher, men built ramps of mud so that the stones could be pulled up to the next level. There they were shifted precisely into position, probably using stone wedges. Once the pyramid was complete, the ramps were taken away.

▼ This painted relief is from a tomb at Saqqara belonging to Ti, a pyramid foreman. It is famous for its craft scenes. This scene shows shipbuilding in progress. Boats were essential for transporting materials to the pyramid-building sites.

One man splits timber using a weight

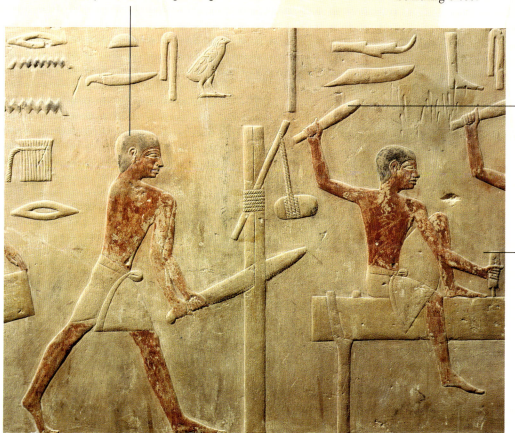

Ancient Egyptians had no mechanical tools to help them

This man is hammering in a drill

Trade and empire

The Egypt of the pharaohs lasted for 3000 years. Throughout that vast period, Egyptian power in the region grew and faded many times. The final era of expansion came at the end of the New Kingdom. The Nineteenth **Dynasty** produced two great military leaders, Seti I and Rameses II. Their campaigns once again established Egyptian control in Nubia, and in about 1275 BC brought peace with the aggressive Hittites of Syria.

Imports and exports

Egypt fought to drive out invaders and to prevent neighbouring peoples from causing trouble on the borders. The Libyans, for example, made raids into Egypt because they wanted to settle on its land. Egypt also fought to get access to important sources of valuable materials. The mines of Nubia in the south supplied most of Egypt's gold, and the area was also rich in copper, **ivory** and even panther skins.

Trade did not just depend on conquest. Since the earliest times, Egyptian merchants had travelled to nearby countries, and foreign ships and donkey caravans had brought in goods from many parts of the world. Tomb paintings from Beni Hasan show traders from Palestine and the Middle East, bringing cosmetics, metal weapons and leather products. Fragments of pottery from Greece have been found in Egypt, and

▼ This piece of jewellery, found in the tomb of Tutankhamen, is known as a pectoral. It originally hung around the king's neck on a cord. It is of a **scarab** beetle, a symbol sacred to the sun god, and it holds a sun disc in its front legs.

Disc representing the sun

Lapis lazuli, imported from Afghanistan

Turquoise, mined in deserts to the east

Winged scarab beetle, made of lapis lazuli set in gold

Gold setting for the stones and glass

some influence of Greek artists can be seen in Egyptian art of the Amarna period. Precious stones for jewellery – such as amethyst, lapis lazuli and turquoise – came from as far away as Afghanistan.

▶ The decoration on this base of a colossal statue of Rameses III symbolizes the king defeating the enemies of Egypt. The king's name, enclosed in a cartouche (oval shape in the centre), has been given arms, with which it grasps the hair of the enemies. Showing Egypt's enemies on the statue base in this way suggests the king is treading them underfoot, defeated.

Images of the enemy

Many paintings and carvings give detailed pictures of Egypt's enemies being defeated, captured or killed. The traditional foes, such as the Libyans and Nubians, were often shown as bound and helpless captives, their images set into the pavements of temples and palaces (and even the soles of the king's sandals) so that they would be trodden on.

The Egyptian army

The shock of the invasions by the Hyksos at the end of the Middle Kingdom had made the later kings determined to improve the training and weapons of the Egyptian army. They copied many of the techniques of the Asiatic soldiers. New Kingdom archers used a **composite bow** made of layers of horn and wood, which was more powerful than previous weapons. Many were now carried into battle in chariots, driven by expert warriors. Foot soldiers wielded maces, battleaxes, spears and **bronze** swords.

Egypt never had a regular navy, but at the end of the New Kingdom fleets of ships were organized to meet attacks by the 'Sea Peoples' (Mediterranean pirates and settlers). When Rameses III fought a great battle against them at the mouth of the Nile, the Egyptians forced the Sea Peoples' boats into narrow inlets in the **delta**, where archers fired upon them from the shore. Details of the pharaoh's victory are carved at the entrance to his mortuary temple at Medinet Habu.

▼ This is a model dating to the Middle Kingdom and found in the tomb of a man called Mesheti. It is one of two models depicting Egyptian soldiers, in this case spearmen. It shows a large detachment of men, all individually carved from wood.

These spears have a bronze tip mounted on a wooden shaft

The original shields were of wood covered in cow hide

The soldiers are carved marching in step

Soldiers have bare feet

Simple white kilt worn at the waist

Valley of the Kings

The Egyptians described the royal tombs as 'mansions of eternity'. They should remain complete and sealed, a symbol that the dead kings inside were still alive in the afterlife, and watching over their people. The pyramids were very obvious monuments, however, and robbers knew that they contained wonderful treasures. Over the centuries, these tombs were ransacked, and by the time of the New Kingdom, kings had decided to be buried somewhere much more secret.

Hidden chambers

A remote valley near Thebes was chosen, in the cliffs on the west bank of the Nile marked by a pyramid-shaped peak. Here, the tombs for the kings were dug down into the rock, with long passages running deep underground.

The passages passed through a series of halls before reaching the burial chamber itself, a dark and silent room which must have seemed a model of the underworld.

From outside, the tombs were invisible. Inside many were beautifully decorated with wall paintings and carved reliefs. The tomb of Seti I (rediscovered in 1817) was especially magnificent, with a vividly painted corridor leading to a hall with columns, a chamber, and then to the burial chamber itself. Amongst its marvels was a huge ceiling painted with the night sky and gold stars, and an intricately carved **alabaster** coffin that was so thin it was transparent.

▼ Part of the eerily painted ceiling in the burial chamber of King Seti I in the Valley of the Kings. It depicts the night sky and the constellations, signified using mythological beasts and gods.

Night sky is painted a deep blue

Figures are painted gold

Stars are shown as red dots on the figures

Ancient Egyptian constellations were different from the ones we describe today

There are a number of unidentifiable deities, some with human heads, some with animal heads

Tomb robbers

Over the next 500 years, all the Egyptian kings were buried here. Many of the tombs were packed with precious objects, such as fine clothes and perfumes, gold weapons, jewellery and **gilded** furniture. The entrances were sealed and carefully hidden. But robbers still found their way in, sometimes within days of the funeral. They stole whatever they could sell and often smashed the rest. Some were arrested and put on trial.

The best-known tomb in the Valley of the Kings is also one of the smallest. Tutankhamen's burial place somehow escaped the ransacking of the robber gangs, although some did break in and make a mess, but took little. In 1922, Howard Carter saw the jumble of treasures for the first time, and he was astonished. 'At first I could see nothing,' he wrote, 'the hot air escaping from the chamber causing the candle flame to flicker, but presently details of the room emerged from the mist; strange animals, statues and gold – everywhere the glint of gold.'

▼ A replica of the antechamber of Tutankhamen's tomb. The antechamber was the largest room and the last the body was taken through before it was placed in the burial chamber at the rear. The room is filled with precious objects.

Many chests, chairs and beds filled the room

The entrance door to the burial chamber

Statues are painted black, with gold kilts and headdresses

Three huge gilded beds, shaped like animals: a hippo, a cow and a cheetah

Body of a chariot

Life-size guardian statues stand on either side of the door

Deir el-Medina

To try to keep the secret of the Valley of the Kings, a special village was built for the site workers, called Deir el-Medina. Here the workers were cut off from the outside world. The kings paid them with food and water, employing teams of fishermen to bring them fish, and people to do their laundry. The builders worked a 10-hour day, spending the night in shelters near the tombs before going home to their families.

◄ Remains of the workmen's village of Deir el-Medina, on the west bank of the Nile, are hidden under the cliffs about 3 kilometres (2 miles) from the ancient city of Thebes. Seen here are some of the tombs, and just visible in the centre is a small restored pyramid.

Greeks and Romans

Rameses IV was the last great ruler. When he died in about 1158 BC the Egyptian Empire began to collapse for the last time. For a long period, different parts of Egypt were controlled by its neighbours and other invaders. The Persians ruled Egypt for nearly 200 years. Greeks, Jews and Phoenicians also came from across the Mediterranean to live in the country. This invasion inspired the Egyptians to revive the great artistic styles of their past. Temples and other sites were restored, and powerful families bought and decorated burial places near the ancient pyramids.

In 332 BC an entire Greek army arrived, led by Alexander the Great, which drove out the hated Persians. Although Alexander spent very little time in Egypt, he had a huge impact on the country. He founded a great new city at the mouth of the Nile, which he called Alexandria. It became a centre for Hellenistic (Greek) culture, with the very first museum and the biggest library in the world.

The Pharos lighthouse

Outside the harbour of Alexandria was an island called Pharos, and here in about 260 BC the Egyptians and Greeks built one of the **Seven Wonders of the World**. It was an enormous lighthouse, over 120 metres high, with a beacon fire burning at the top night and day to guide ships into the harbour.

▼ An 18th-century engraving of the lighthouse on Pharos. The structure was severely damaged in an earthquake after standing for 1500 years.

The beacon, which guided boats into the harbour, was a fire in a metal basket. The light was probably focused by a system of mirrors, and could be seen over 50 km (30 miles) away

The wood was lifted by a hoist to the very top

The walls of the Pharos were made of white marble

The port of Alexandria

Wood for the fire was drawn up spiral ramps inside by horse and cart

Cleopatra and the Romans

After Alexander's death, the Egyptian throne was seized by Ptolemy, one of his generals. He founded a new dynasty, which was named after him, but holding on to power was increasingly hard. His descendant Ptolemy XII was forced to rely on help from the Romans, who were the new power in the Mediterranean.

▼ This famous carving in hard green stone (called schist) is known as the 'Green Head'. It was produced in about 300 BC. Archaeologists think it shows the head of a priest. It is much more naturalistic than most Egyptian art. The artist is clearly trying to convey the subject's personality. Although we do not know who the man was, he was clearly someone of very high status.

After Ptolemy XII came the most famous of all Egyptian queens, Cleopatra. She dreamed of using the might of Rome to regain control of Egypt's lost territories. When Julius Caesar came to Alexandria in 48 BC she made an alliance with him. After his death Cleopatra quickly became the lover of Mark Antony, one of the new Roman leaders. But the affair caused a political storm in Rome, and then there was war.

The Egyptians were defeated, and the Romans took complete charge of Egypt. They saw it as a rich land that could be used to grow grain for the people of Rome, and introduced a new system of taxation which was even harsher than that of the pharaohs. The final blow fell in AD 383, by which time most of the Roman Empire had become Christian. Emperor Theodosius ordered that all pagan temples should be closed, and the images of the old gods destroyed. The **civilization** of the ancient Egyptians died along with their religion.

▼ Alexander worshipped the Egyptian god Amun, treating him as an equal with the Greek god Zeus. This silver coin, issued *c*. 280 BC, shows the head of Alexander wearing the horn symbol of Zeus-Amun.

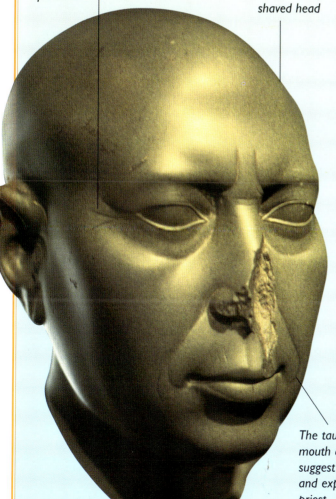

Realistic creases around the eyes and mouth are rarely seen in Egyptian portraits

The man, probably an official or a priest, has a shaved head

The taut lines of the mouth and eyebrows suggest the age, wisdom and experience of the priest

Everyday life

gyptians saw the family unit as vitally important, and put it at the centre of many religious **rituals**. A man was expected to marry and have children as soon as he could. This was crucial for his own afterlife. When he died, his spirit would live on with his corpse, but only as long as his tomb was properly looked after. The children had a duty to arrange the funeral, make the right offerings and tend their father's spirit.

Women and children

Tomb images suggest that women often had large families. In fact many children died very young, but each one was pictured on the tomb as if it had survived. Many pictures also portray the goddess Isis as the perfect mother, suckling her baby son Horus. Mothers often breastfed their infants until they were three years old.

The wife was in charge of the household. This involved a lot of work, from baking the bread and brewing the beer to grinding the grain and washing the clothes. Many of these tasks required a great deal of water, which had to be carried from the nearest well or canal. Hygiene was a frequent problem, for there was little drainage, and household rubbish was thrown on a dump or in the river. Rats, flies and disease could thrive in the hot climate.

Few children were given a formal education. As soon as they were big enough, most worked with their parents in the fields or the workshop. Only the sons of wealthy parents were sent to school.

▼ The dwarf Seneb was a royal tutor during the Old Kingdom period. This family group, showing him with his wife and two children, dates from about 2530 BC. It was carved from limestone and coloured with paint.

The statue was originally sealed up on the tomb in a block of stone, which can be seen behind the sculpture

The position of Seneb's wife's arms is typical. She is shown in a supportive role, with her arms around her husband

Unusually, Seneb's wife is portrayed the same size as her husband

Seneb and his son are painted in red ochre

Seneb's restricted growth can be seen in the short arms and legs (folded beneath him), and the large head and body

The son wears a sidelock of hair, showing he was still very young

The children are cleverly positioned in the place where Seneb's legs might have gone

His wife's skin is painted yellow ochre, as is that of her daughter

▶ Egyptian children usually had toys made from everyday materials. The simplest kind of doll was cut from a flat piece of board. These two figures are sometimes called dolls, but it is not known if they were children's toys or, as is more likely, some sort of fertility object.

The doll has no face

Wigs made of beads

They are made of wood, but have no legs and only rudimentary arms

The bodies are covered in markings, which may or may not be tattoos, or marks made using henna paint

Houses and villas

The rich and powerful were also the only Egyptians who could afford to commission paintings and sculpture, so most of the images that have survived show scenes from better-off households. Courtiers and senior officials often built large villas in the countryside, with many rooms, some lavishly decorated with wall paintings. Outside, there was plenty of space for servants' quarters, fish ponds, orchards and a family shrine.

Most houses were made of mud brick. A craftsman might have a home with four or five rooms, one of which would be the workshop. The rooms were on the ground floor, grouped around a central yard. There was a staircase up to the roof, which was often the coolest place. The poorest people lived in small huts, with their animals kept in a shelter under or beside the main rooms.

▶ A fine wooden statuette of a noble woman made in the Eighteenth **Dynasty**. The woman wears an enormous, finely plaited wig, typical of this period. She has a gold collar and wears an elaborately pleated dress.

Hair dressing

Both men and women treated their hair with scented lotions and often dyed it. Most women liked to keep their hair long, and took a lot of trouble to dress it ornately. They combed it with **ivory** combs and held curls in place with pins and beeswax. However, many Egyptian men and women had shaved heads or very short hair, and for special occasions wore wigs of human hair, or hair pieces if they could not afford full wigs.

Eating and drinking

The Nile valley was a perfect place to grow crops. The annual flooding brought moisture and nutrients to the soil, and the sun gave warmth. The Egyptians made the best possible use of these forces of nature. They kept careful watch on the rising waters of the river. They diverted the natural flow of the Nile on to farmland through **irrigation** channels.

The grain of life

Grain was the most important of the growing crops. The Egyptians referred to it as 'the life-giver', and it was turned into their staple foods of bread and beer. For bread, women ground wheat grains into flour between stones, and made a dough with a yeast mixture, milk and salt. The loaves were shaped and then baked. Lists from funeral inscriptions from the New Kingdom period mention at least 40 different types of bread.

Beer was made from barley grains, which were first mixed into a dough and partly baked into a kind of loaf. The sticky mixture was mashed up again with warm water and left to ferment before being pushed through a sieve and the liquid stored in jars. The result was flat and cloudy, though the taste could be improved by flavouring it with spices or dates.

▶ Workers harvest grapes and then tread them to make wine, in this painted **relief** from the tomb of Nakht, *c.*1350 BC. Only the rich could afford to drink wine made from grapes. Poorer people drank beer, or wine made from other fruits such as pomegranates.

▶ This limestone carving from Saqqara, dating from the Old Kingdom, shows very thin, starving men. It is believed to be evidence of a famine.

Famine and disease

The only times that people went hungry were in the rare and terrible periods of drought or disease. If the Nile failed to rise high enough, it did not irrigate the fields and the plants withered in the harsh sun, meaning there was not enough grain for Egyptians to eat. Fatal diseases such as dysentery and typhoid were also a regular danger.

Tapered clay vessels for storing the wine while it ferments

The grape vines are grown in high arches

The grapes are heaped in a vat and then crushed by trampling them underfoot

Draining off the grape juice into a basin

Cookery and mealtimes

Ordinary Egyptians cooked their food on a hearth-stone set in an open fire, or in a simple round oven made of baked clay, using dried animal dung or straw as the main fuel. There were few trees in the land, and the cutting of firewood was tightly controlled, so only richer people with big kitchens could afford to burn wood. Much of the food was stewed and would include meat (mainly goat, beef or mutton) or fish, and vegetables such as onions and leeks. Egyptians ate three meals a day. Tables were rare: the family sat on a large rush mat, helping themselves to the food from a dish placed in the centre.

Hunting and fishing

There are many scenes of hunting wild game in Egyptian art. This was mainly a pastime for kings and the upper classes, and some animals could be hunted only by royalty. Paintings show kings hurling throw sticks at water birds, or using hounds to chase bulls, gazelles or even lions in the desert. Fish, usually caught with nets by full-time hunters, were also an important source of food.

▼ This wall painting from the tomb of Nebamun, a government official, shows Nebamun out hunting on the Nile marshes with his family. The animals and plants were painted realistically and in great detail, with ingenious use of a limited range of colours.

Nebamun is the biggest figure in the painting

Many species of ducks and other water birds

Throw stick, ready to hurl at the water birds which fly out of the reeds

A cat fetches the birds which are knocked down

Nebamun's wife is a much smaller figure than him, dressed in a fine gown and carrying a bouquet of flowers

Papyrus reeds on the edge of the river

Nebamun stands on a papyrus raft

The river is rich in big fish

Nebamun's daughter is the smallest figure. She gathers lotus flowers from the water

At work

Egypt was one of the most densely populated countries of the ancient world. During the New Kingdom period, there were more than three million people in the Nile valley. The vast majority of these lived in settlements in the countryside, where they worked in the fields or in workshops. Everyone (except courtiers and, of course, the king) had to work for a living. On the lowest level were the unskilled workers, such as peasant labourers, while above them came the small tradesmen, including farmers, builders, merchants and craftsmen of all kinds.

▼ This wall painting shows a farmer driving his herd of cattle. Egyptians kept cows for their meat and leather, although beef was reserved for wealthy people and others rarely tasted it.

On the land

The work of the farmer was bound to the rise and fall of the Nile, and thus with the gods of the river, the seasons and fertility. The annual rituals of farming are celebrated in many Egyptian paintings and texts. When the floods subsided, labourers moved onto the black-silted land, repairing ditches, clearing weeds, ploughing the soil and sowing seeds.

Tax officials measured the crop and calculated how much tax each farmer would have to pay. After harvest, the ears of maize were spread on the ground to dry and then trampled by oxen or hit with flails to break open the husks. The farmer 'winnowed' the maize by throwing it into the air with wooden fans and letting the lighter husks blow away in the wind. Richer farmers also kept large herds of cattle, who grazed on the pastures alongside the river.

A painted line of **hieroglyphs** accompanies the scene

Cow hide was an important material, used for making everything from chair seats to war shields

The artist has painted the different colours and patterns of the cow hides. The cows are more naturalistic than is usual

▶ A pair of carpenters make a **gilded** wooden shrine decorated with **amulets** (charms), in this wall painting from a tomb of the New Kingdom period.

*A chisel-shaped tool, probably of copper or **bronze***

Amulets

Craft workers

Egyptian craftsmen were highly skilled, using just simple materials. Potters made a huge range of things with the clay and silt from the riverbanks, from plain everyday bowls to intricately painted jars. Locally quarried stone, such as **basalt** which is very hard, was carved into vessels to be buried in tombs or used in religious ceremonies.

Carpenters had simple tools, much like the ones we use today, and preferred to work with cedar and other timber imported from Phoenicia or Lebanon. Even without iron for fixings, they made beautiful furniture and coffins, as well as much larger objects such as ships and chariots. Their tools were manufactured by metalworkers, who also produced ornaments in hammered gold sheet, decorating them by pressing patterns into the gold.

▶ A black **granite** statue of Sennufer (mayor of Thebes in about 1395 BC) with his wife and daughter. Their daughter is shown much smaller. Sennofer wears a long kilt. Around his neck is a huge collar made of discs, known as a shebu collar, which was awarded by the king to faithful servants. He is shown with rolls of fat around his waist. Being overweight was a sign of status and affluence. His wife, who has one arm around her husband, wears a heavy wig and a long, tightly fitting dress.

Sculptors

There was no single word for 'artist' in ancient Egypt. Sculptors (as well as painters) were seen as skilled craft workers, whose job was not to create beautiful decorations but to provide images to go with the words of inscriptions on tombs, temples and other structures. However, there were several words for 'sculptor'. One of these translates as 'he who keeps alive' – someone who preserved his subject as a living person in stone.

Entertainment

Egyptians spent much of their time working, but they still had some hours in the week to enjoy themselves. A **vizier** of the Old Kingdom, called Ptah-hotep, gave this advice: 'Do not shorten the time devoted to pleasure. When your fortune is made, follow your desire; for a fortune is no good if you are glum.' Many of their leisure pursuits, from banquets to spectator sports and country outings, can be seen pictured on tomb walls.

Music and dance

Musicians are often given a special place in paintings of feasts and funeral rituals. Music and dance played an important part in temple worship, but they were also enjoyed as entertainment at family gatherings, feasts and parties. The main stringed instruments were the harp and the lute, which had sound boxes made of wood or a tortoise shell. Flutes and other wind instruments were of reed or metal. A simple drum made of palm wood with a stretched skin cover has been discovered in a Middle Kingdom tomb.

Dance performances sometimes featured young girls, who moved gracefully together in complex patterns. Other paintings show male and female dancers in two rows, with their arms held out. The dancers and audience kept time by shaking tambourines, clicking wooden clappers, or stamping their feet. The entertainment might also include choirs of singers, and teams of acrobats.

▼ Three girls entertain diners at a banquet by playing music on a variety of instruments. This scene is in the tomb of Nakht, who was a royal gardener in about 1350 BC. The figures are painted in such a way that almost seems to show movement, and one can imagine them swaying to the rhythm of their music.

Pipes made from two reeds joined together at the mouthpiece

A form of lute

All have long hair, or wigs and headbands

The player is scantily clothed, suggesting she was probably a dancer as well

A tall harp, which stood on the floor

Toys, pets and games

Children had all kinds of toys that we would recognize today. They played with leather balls stuffed with straw, clay dolls, rattles made of dried gourds (a kind of vegetable), and carved wooden models of horses, hippos and other animals. Many households also kept real animals as pets, including monkeys, geese and of course dogs and cats. Some people even asked that their favourite dog or cat should be mummified and placed inside the tomb when they were buried.

In the evenings, families might sit on their rooftops and play games with boards, dice and marbles. Some of these games are the oldest ever devised. The most popular was called senet, in which two players moved their pieces on a board with 30 squares. Some senet sets were very elaborate (three ornate ones were found in the tomb of Tutankhamen), but the game could also be played on an outline scratched in the earth.

▼ A modern facsimile of a Theban tomb painting, showing a New Kingdom government official and his wife playing senet together. They both wear elaborate pleated linen robes, fine wigs and expensive jewellery, showing they are wealthy and of high status.

▼ This game board is one of several found in Tutankhamen's tomb. It is very small, and is carved of ivory which has been stained. The game was played by two players (not the two shapes of pieces), and the idea seems to have been a race around the board, with the first one to get all their pieces off being the winner. Throw sticks served as dice.

Light and dark pieces. The two sets also have different shapes

Drawer for storing pieces underneath

The hieroglyphs mark this set as belonging to the king and give his names and titles

▼ Fighting displays were conducted at festivals for the pleasure of the king. This carving from the tomb of Kheruef shows soldiers fighting.

Woman has her arm around her husband

Sceptre, indicating his important official position

The man wonders where to place the next piece

The senet board on a table

Elaborate cushions on the chairs

The pet cat sits beneath the stool

Wrestlers and stick fighters

The tomb of Kheruef, a royal steward of the Eighteenth Dynasty, contains graphic carvings of a festival he organized for the **pharaoh**. Among the many dramatic scenes are images of men wrestling and fighting with sticks. These fights were a very popular part of grand entertainments, and featured fighters who were clearly skilled and highly trained.

Scribes and hieroglyphs

Writing developed very early in Egypt's history. Once the dynasties of pharaohs were established, officials wanted to be able to record information such as the dates of reigns, the names of kings and queens, important events and calculations of tax. Two things were needed: a system of signs to use, and trained scribes to do the actual writing.

The god's words

Thoth was not just the Egyptian god of wisdom, but also the gods' scribe. People believed that the system of hieroglyphs had been invented by him, so the written language was actually 'the god's words'. They were used for everything from labelling jars and telling stories to setting down laws and inscribing prayers.

Instead of letters, hieroglyphs used symbols that conveyed different sounds and ideas. The earliest signs were simple pictures of things which Egyptians could easily recognize, such as animals, people and everyday objects. But the writing also had to express more complex things – ideas and abstract actions such as thinking or loving. So another kind of hieroglyphic symbol was developed, using sounds instead of pictures. By combining the two types of sign, scribes could construct many new words.

▼ Part of the papyrus known as the *Book of the Dead*, showing hieroglyphic texts. These papyri were a set of instructions on how to enter the afterlife and confront all the **deities** and demons on the journey.

The text is written in an abbreviated or cursive form of hieroglyph

The pictures depict some of the many deities of the afterlife

Scribes usually did their work on strong and long-lasting papyrus

This type of papyrus is often illustrated, depending on the wealth and status of the deceased

▶ Part of a large scene in which a scribe records details of the year's harvest. Scribes kept their paints and tools in a wooden case beside them. The scribe dipped his pen or brush (often made of a piece of reed with a frayed tip) into a clay bowl of water, then rubbed it onto one of the dried cakes of **pigment** to load the colour.

Wooden palette to hold his reed pens, with two hollows for holding the colours he needed for writing: red and black

The scribe wears a white kilt

He wears a long robe, which the artist has shown to be semi-transparent

Training to be a scribe

The writing of hieroglyphs was a central part of Egyptian art, requiring the skill and talent of a painter. This meant that it was seen as a craft that had to be carefully and thoroughly learned. Usually only boys from rich or influential families went through the long training. At the age of ten they went to a scribal school, often run by the priests at the local temple.

The work must have been dull and hard. Pupils had to begin learning the hundreds of different signs; some believe there were more than 800. They practised their writing on plain tablets of clay, or on fragments of clay pots called *ostraca*, on which it was easy to rub out mistakes. After they finished school they went on to work for a master scribe, or joined a temple training college where they learned specialized skills.

Scribes and their work

A qualified scribe was a highly respected member of Egyptian society. He might be employed by the king to inscribe royal documents or record expeditions, by a temple to write funerary texts, or by a local community to record river levels and cattle numbers. He had a responsible job, and the connection with Thoth gave him respect. Scribes were also well paid: one text said, 'No scribe is short of food or of riches from the palace.'

Religion and mythology

The Egyptians developed many different religious beliefs which explained to them how the world worked. Egypt itself lay at the centre, rising up from the waters of Nun, or chaos. Every morning the Sun rose out of the water – this was the god Re, who crossed the sky above the Earth in his sacred boat, and then returned to the underworld at night. Other myths said that a giant **scarab** beetle rolled the Sun across the sky. These and many other myths were pictured again and again in tomb paintings and carvings.

Maat

At the centre of Egyptian life was a belief in truth, justice and harmony, and a world in which everything had its proper place. These ideas came together in the word 'maat', which represented the delicate balance that prevented disasters such as famine or war.

▼ Part of a **papyrus**, showing the judgement of the dead. The god Thoth records the weighing of a dead person's heart against a feather, representing *maat* (or truth).

Some of the many gods of the underworld, who sit in judgement

Anubis leads the dead man

Ammit 'the devourer' (a beast, part crocodile, hippo and lion) stands ready to devour the heart if the dead man does not pass the test

Thoth, with the head of an **ibis**, records the verdict

The dead man is led before Osiris

Isis and Nephthys (protector of the dead)

Creation myths

The Egyptians had several stories about how the gods first appeared. One told how Atum, the creator god, caused the mound of earth to rise above the dark ocean of chaos. Nun put on it two gods, one for the air and one for the water. They gave birth to Geb, god of the earth, and Nut, goddess of the sky, who in their turn had four children.

Among these children were Osiris, the well-loved god of farming and fertility, and his jealous brother Seth, ruler of storms and the barren desert. The violent Seth killed Osiris, chopped his body into pieces and scattered them in the Nile, which carried them all over Egypt. His sister Isis patiently travelled through the land to find all the body parts and put Osiris back together. By reciting special prayers, Isis brought the body to life again, then Osiris was welcomed into the underworld where he came to rule the dead.

Gods and goddesses

Egyptian mythology can be very confusing, because gods changed and merged over time. However, there were several major **deities** (besides those already mentioned) whose importance changed little over the centuries. Horus was the son of Osiris, who came to represent the spirit of the **pharaoh** whilst he was alive. Horus was identified with the **falcon**. Sekhmet was the terrible goddess of war and vengeance, who is shown with the head of a lioness. Anubis was the 'lord of the graveyard' who watched over the dead and prepared them for embalming. He is shown with a jackal's head. Thoth was the god of learning and wisdom, and patron of scribes. He is shown with the head of an ibis. Amun was unknown in the Old Kingdom, but he was later worshipped as 'king of the gods'. Amun became merged with Re, the old Sun god.

The god Anubis or, more likely, a priest wearing a mask representing the jackal-headed god

▶ A scene from a tomb at Deir el-Medina village, depicting the mummy of Sennedjem. The wrapped mummy has a portrait mask, showing Sennedjem with a long wig and a false beard.

Embalming was done in a tented area. Here there are tent poles at either side and some patterned fabric hanging from them

The body lies on a bed in the shape of a lion or cheetah, with the animal's head at one end and the long tail at the other

The painted outer coffin

37

Mummification

The death of a pharaoh was always a crucial moment in Egyptian history. Not only did a new ruler have to be crowned, but the old king had to be ushered into the underworld with the correct **rituals**. Egyptians believed that a pharaoh was a god, and a descendant of the first god-king Osiris. When he was on the throne, he was the embodiment of the god Horus (Osiris' son), and when he died he became Osiris himself. He would therefore continue to protect and serve Egypt after death.

▶ The gold mask of Tutankhamen, now in the Cairo Museum. The king's mummy was enclosed in three coffins, but the mummy itself had this splendid funerary mask which covered the entire upper body. The face is believed to be a good likeness of the king.

Tomb and temple

The long process of burial began at once with the journey of the royal corpse to its tomb. In Old Kingdom times (and some of the Middle Kingdom), this would have been a pyramid, though New Kingdom pharaohs were buried underground in the Valley of the Kings. Attendants wrapped the body in cloths and laid it on a funeral barge.

Priests guarded the corpse as the barge moved across the Nile and up a specially built canal to the pyramid complex. They travelled east to west, copying the course of the Sun on its daily journey into the underworld. The king's body was unloaded at a stone jetty and carried into the 'valley temple', the lowest room of the complex, ready to be embalmed.

Protective divinities – the vulture and cobra goddesses

The king's ears are pierced, though these piercings were covered up when the mask was first revealed

A wide collar, which ends with hawk heads on the shoulders

The false beard of Osiris, the god of the dead, in this instance made of gold inlaid with lapis lazuli

The eyes are made of obsidian and quartz, outlined in blue glass

*Striped **nemes** headdress, gold with blue stripes of coloured glass*

The rows are made up of beads of carnelian, turquoise and coloured glass

Preserving body and spirit

Why did the Egyptians mummify their dead kings? Obviously it was a perfect method of preserving a body, but the process also had deep religious meaning, always spelled out by tomb paintings. The body of Osiris had been cut to pieces, then put together again and returned to life in the underworld. The wrapping of the king's body was an imitation of this, in preparation for his life after death.

Egyptians believed that the spirit was released when a person died. The spirit has two essential parts: the *ka*, or life force, and the *ba*, the person's individual character. These two spirits could only live on if the dead body was properly preserved, for the *ba* made a daily journey out of the tomb into the underworld, while the *ka* stayed with the body. If the body rotted away, the *ba* would have nowhere to return to at night.

▼ This is a scene showing the Sun god Re travelling the heavens accompanied by other gods. This painted **relief** carving was found in the tomb of King Seti I in the Valley of the Kings.

| Oars for steering the boat | Re carries an ankh symbol, the symbol of life, and a staff | The Sun god Re, as a ram-headed deity | The goddess Hathor, wearing her cow-horn headdress which holds a sun disc | Hooded cobras sit in the bows of the boat to protect the king |

▼ **Canopic jars**, decorated with heads, which held the vital organs (liver, lungs, intestines and stomach) taken from a mummified body. These jars are carved from stone.

Embalmers at work

Embalmers at the valley temple had a very delicate and complicated job to do. Watched closely by priests, and with the chanting of religious texts echoing round the workshop, they laid the corpse on a table. They then removed the brain via the nose, and took out the stomach, lungs and other important organs. After washing out and disinfecting the empty corpse with palm wine, they covered it in a kind of salt called natron to draw out the moisture. The dried body was then packed with linen and spices and wrapped in linen strips (some mummies were bound with more than 2000 metres of this). Priests placed **amulets** (charms) and jewels in the folds of the linen.

Burial

The great tombs of the pharaohs were built as houses of eternity. The vast pyramids made of stone blocks, and the secret halls and passages dug into the valleys, were meant to last undamaged for ever, the permanent home where the old king could live on. They were deeply sacred places. One tomb inscription reads: 'Whoever damages any stone or brick of this tomb of mine, I shall seize by the neck like a bird, and I shall make him so terrified that all living people and spirits will see him and be afraid.'

▼ A group of women mourners in a funeral procession. These women were probably not family members, but were professional mourners (with one very young girl as an apprentice) paid to perform at the funeral. They would wail, cry and place ashes on their heads – something that still happens in Egypt today.

Into the tomb

Religious texts stated that the preparation of the body should take 70 days. Then the bearers placed the body in a wooden coffin, which was often decorated with **gilding** and painted figures. The coffin was lifted onto a sledge, and hauled by ropes out of the valley temple and up a long sloping causeway to the funerary temple at the side of the pyramid. Here the priests performed the funeral rituals, reciting texts and offering perfumes, food and wine to the gods.

The coffin continued its journey out of the temple and into the pyramid itself. Behind it came a long procession of mourners, family relatives and priests. Among them might be the pharaoh's widow and another woman, dressed as the goddesses Isis and Nephthys who originally prayed over the body of Osiris.

Man carrying a piece of furniture, possibly a chest

Their faces show real sorrow. They are all crying, and lines running from the eyes indicate where their black eye-liner has run

They raise their arms in the air

Men carrying floral garlands and objects for the tomb

The burial chamber

The procession moved through a maze of low-ceilinged tunnels into the burial chamber at the heart of the pyramid. The bearers placed the wooden coffin inside a second coffin, usually made of stone. This was the sarcophagus, which was magnificently carved and gilded, and had a heavy stone lid. After a final reading, and the placing of food, drink, treasures and personal possessions around the sarcophagus, everyone left the chamber. The doors were sealed so that no one could ever enter again.

No one, that is, except for the dead pharaoh. Egyptians believed that he lived on inside the tomb, still watching over the land and its people. Statues of the pharaoh were placed by the sarcophagus to show that he was still alive. Each morning the *ba* spirit left the tomb in the form of a bird to journey across the sky with the Sun and down into the underworld, and each night it returned.

▼ An end view of the sarcophagus of King Tuthmose IV, from his tomb in the Valley of the Kings. Carved from pink quarzite stone, it dates from about 1386 BC.

The lid of the sarcophagus. It shows damage from where ancient tomb robbers forced it open with tools

The goddess Nephthys, who protected the dead, spreads her arms upwards in a guarding position

Religious texts cut into the stone

► This gilded wood shield is one of eight shields found in the tomb of Tutankhamen. It shows the king about to kill a lion with a curved sword. Above the king is a winged sun disc, representing the sun god, and the king wears the headdress of Amun-Re. A vulture, one of the protective deities of the king, sits behind him.

Grave goods

The burial chamber was crammed with objects that the pharaoh would need in the afterlife. Many of these were practical – chests of food and clothing, oils and scents, chairs and even weapons; others were symbols of wealth and magic. The chamber of Tutankhamen contained golden chariots, animal carvings and trumpets, as well as fabulous jewellery.

Priests and rituals

Each god (and therefore each dead pharaoh) had a temple dedicated to their worship. This might be a humble mud-brick building or an enormous cluster of courtyards and halls like the Temple of Amun at Karnak, depending on the god's importance. The outer courts were open to the public on special days, but only a king or priest could enter the outer rooms or the central shrine where the god was believed to live. The temple was often the economic centre of a community, employing local people to work the estates, offices and kitchens.

▼ Two statues of Rameses II in the Temple of Amun at Karnak. The open courtyard is surrounded by columns, and between these were larger-than-life-sized statues of the king, of which these are the best preserved.

Inside the temple

The temple reflected the way the Egyptians saw the universe. Around the sacred complex was a mud-brick wall which separated it from the chaos of the world outside. The wall was covered with carvings of the country's victories over its enemies. Inside was a pillared hallway: the pillars represented the papyrus reeds of the Nile, while the ceiling above was painted to show the night sky.

To reach the inner shrine at the heart of the temple, the priests walked up a sloping floor. This symbolized the original mound of earth raised out of the waters of chaos by the creator god. The shrine itself was enclosed behind a locked and sealed door. Here stood the statue of the god, usually made of carved and gilded wood, or sometimes of solid gold inlaid with precious stones.

They show a youthful king, standing with his left leg forwards

Nemes headdress and a broad false beard

*Each statue is carved from a single piece of **granite***

He wears a short kilt

He holds a roll of linen in each hand

*This is part of the king's elaborate crown and would have rested on top of the **nemes** headdress*

A priest's life

The temple priests performed their services two or three times every day. The high priest, wearing his ceremonial leopard-skin cloak, broke the mud seal on the shrine door and bowed to the image of the god. There were hymns and prayers of greeting to wake the god, often accompanied by music, and the statue was washed and dressed. Perfumed oils were added.

A priest had a simple but very busy life. He had to make sure that he was completely clean and pure in order to perform the rituals in the shrine. He bathed twice a day, shaved his entire body and wore simple clothes of white linen. Priests worked in teams, who operated in shifts of three months in a year. This meant that they often had other work, as scribes or teachers. Almost all priests were men, although a pharaoh's wife or daughter was sometimes given a senior role as a priestess in temple rituals.

▶ Painted reliefs like this one, from the Temple of Rameses II at Abydos, are some of the best preserved in Egypt. Although all reliefs in temples were painted, usually the paint has not survived. This figure represents the Nile god Hapi, bearing offerings to the gods. He holds three papyrus stems and a large tray heaped with food offerings (bread, ducks, grapes and flowers).

The daily ceremonies

Each day the priest brought the god food and drink to give him energy. This would include bread, roasted meat, fruit and jars of beer or wine (the priests later removed these offerings and probably used them for their own meals). After the ritual, the high priest walked backwards out of the shrine, brushing away his footprints, closed the door and replaced the seal.

▼ This figure is of an Iwnmutef priest. He performs one of the daily ritual offerings at a royal tomb. This wall painting is in the tomb of Rameses IX.

He has a short wig with a plait on one side, known as a side lock, showing he had not reached maturity

The priest holds high a bowl containing an offering to the god, probably water

He is dressed in a panther skin – the mark of a high priest

The panther's tail

Timeline

BC
Period up to the First Dynasty (dates approximate)

17,000
first settlers arrive in Egypt

14,000
climate of the region becomes hotter and drier: desert advances and settlements cluster in Nile valley

5000
small communities grow up along the River Nile

3100
King Menes/Narmer unites Upper and Lower Egypt, and becomes the first **pharaoh**

3050
First **Dynasty** of rulers established

Old Kingdom

2686
Third Dynasty of rulers begins what is called the Old Kingdom period

2660
Djoser orders building the Step Pyramid at Saqqara – the first major stone monument

2580
Khufu orders building the Great Pyramid at Giza

2450
Re becomes a major national god

2180–2040
First Intermediate period, with the fall of the Old Kingdom, due to rise in power of local *nomarchs* (governors) and a possible famine

Middle Kingdom

2040
Egypt reunited under Mentuhotep II (Eleventh Dynasty): start of what is now called the Middle Kingdom period

c.1990
building work begins on the Temple of Amun at Karnak

c.1860
Sesostris III (Twelfth Dynasty) masterminds construction of forts to deter invaders from north and south

1782–1570
Second Intermediate period, includes collapse of pharaonic rule and invasion by the Hyksos peoples of Asia

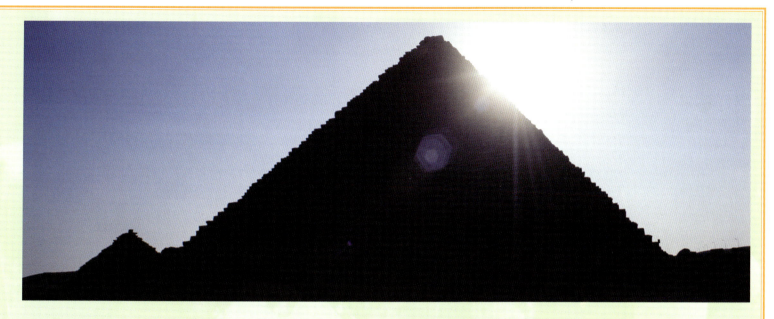

New Kingdom

1570

Ahmose I (Eighteenth Dynasty) completes expulsion of Hyksos: start of what is now called the New Kingdom period

1498

Hatshepsut seizes throne on death of her husband Tuthmose II: orders building of mortuary temple at Luxor

1367

Amenhotep IV becomes pharaoh: changes his name to Akhenaten and establishes worship of Aten in place of other gods: builds new royal city at El-Amarna

1360

on death of Akhenaten, Tutankhamen becomes king at the age of nine

1275

Hittites defeated by Rameses II (Nineteenth Dynasty) at Kadesh in Syria

1200

construction of temple at Abu Simbel begins, to honour Rameses II

1158

death of Rameses III, last of the great pharaohs

1070–525

final decline of Egyptian power during what is called the Third Intermediate period

Foreign rulers

525

Persian King Cambyses defeats Egyptians at Pelusium and takes control of the land

464–454

revolt against Persian rule allows Egyptian kings to seize power

423

Persians regain control

332

Alexander the Great defeats the Persians and founds Alexandria

323

death of Alexander: Ptolemy I starts Greek dynasty

c.290

work begins on building the Pharos lighthouse at Alexandria

51

Cleopatra becomes queen of Egypt on seizing throne from her brother Ptolemy XIII

31

Cleopatra and Mark Antony defeated by Roman army and navy at Actium: Egypt becomes part of the Roman Empire

AD

383

Roman Emperor Theodosius destroys non-Christian places of worship: end of Egyptian religion

Glossary

alabaster hard, cloudy white stone

amulet charm worn to guard against evil

archaeologist person who finds, studies and preserves the remains of ancient civilizations

Art Deco decorative art style that was popular in the 1920s and 1930s

artefact man-made object, especially a tool or weapon

basalt very hard stone formed from the outflow of a volcano

bronze alloy (mixture) of copper and tin, and sometimes other metals

cannibalism the act of a human eating human flesh

canopic jar ritual jar containing the organs (such as stomach and lungs) of a mummified corpse

civil war a war fought between people of the same country

civilization society in advanced state of development

composite bow weapon made from two or more materials (usually wood and horn) glued together to add strength

deity god

delta triangular area at the mouth of a river, formed by the deposit of silt and other materials

dynasty family or line of rulers, who inherit power from each other

ebony hard, black tropical wood

Egyptology study of the language and culture of ancient Egypt

falcon species of hawk with long pointed wings

gild cover with a thin layer of gold

granite hard, coarse-grained rock formed by the heat of volcanic action

hieroglyph the picture writing of ancient Egyptians

hypostyle having a roof resting upon columns, constructed by means of columns

ibis wading bird with long thin legs and a long thin bill

incense substances (usually kinds of gum or spice) that make a pleasant perfume when burned

irrigation delivering water to crops by diverting it from rivers or lakes into channels

ivory hard, white material from the tusks of elephants

mastaba massive mud-brick tombs

nemes striped headdress of pharaohs, which hangs down both sides of the face and shoulder

obelisk tall, four-sided stone pillar, gradually tapering as it rises, pyramidal at the top. Egyptian obelisks are usually covered with hieroglyphs

papyrus early form of paper made from the pressed and woven stems of the papyrus reed

pharaoh title of the ruler of ancient Egypt

pigment colouring matter used as paint or dye

relief method of carving or sculpture in which pictures stand out from the background

ritual special words and actions used at a ceremony, maybe a religious ceremony

scarab species of dung beetle, sacred to the Egyptians

Seven Wonders of the World seven amazing structures from the ancient world: the pyramids of Egypt, the hanging gardens of Babylon, the Temple of Artemis at Ephesus, the statue of Zeus at Olympia, the Mausoleum at Halicarnassus, the Colossus of Rhodes and the Pharos (lighthouse) at Alexandria

sphinx stone figure with a man's or animal's head upon the body of a lion

square building tool with a set right angle for ensuring that corners are exactly square

vizier the pharaoh's chief minister and official, who oversees the daily running of government

Further resources

Books

Aldred, Cyril, *Egyptian Art* (Thames & Hudson, 1980)

Ardagh, Philip, *Hieroglyphs Handbook: Teach Yourself Ancient Egyptian* (Faber, 1999)

Harris, Geraldine, *All in a Day's Work: Pharaohs and Embalmers* (Peter Bedrick, 2001)

Harris, Geraldine and Pemberton, Delia, *Illustrated Encyclopedia of Ancient Egypt* (British Museum, 1999)

Hart, George and others, *Eyewitness: Ancient Egypt* (Dorling Kindersley, 2000)

Morley, Jacqueline and Hewetson, Nick, *Magnifications: The Living Tomb* (Peter Bedrick, 2001)

Netzley, Patricia D., *Greenhaven Encyclopedia of Ancient Egypt* (Greenhaven, 2003)

Ross, Stewart and Bonson, Richard, *Tales of the Dead: Ancient Egypt* (Dorling Kindersley, 2003)

Wilson, Eva, *Pattern Books: Ancient Egyptian Designs* (British Museum, 1986)

Museums

Museums in many countries have important Egyptian exhibits. Among them are:

Agyptisches Museum, Berlin, Germany

Ashmolean Museum, Oxford, UK

British Museum, London, UK

Brooklyn Museum, New York, USA

Field Museum and Oriental Institute of the University of Chicago, Chicago, USA

Louvre, Paris, France

Metropolitan Museum of Art, New York, USA

Museum of Fine Arts, Boston, Massachusetts, USA

Websites

http://www.ancientegypt.co.uk/menu.html

A British Museum site, with information, stories, animations and challenges on many features of ancient Egypt

http://www.bbc.co.uk/history/ancient/egyptians/

Examples of ancient Egyptian art, text and hieroglyphs, with interactive options

http://www.bergen.org/AAST/Projects/Egypt/index.html

Historical facts about ancient Egyptian art and culture

http://www.eyelid.co.uk/index.htm

Mark Millmore's ancient Egypt – facts about kings and queens, temple and pyramid reconstructions, hieroglyphic ecards to send

http://en.wikipedia.org/wiki/Ancient_Egypt

Information on ancient Egypt from Wikipedia, the free encylopedia

Index

Akhenaten, King 14, 15, 45
Alexander the Great 24, 25, 45
Alexandria 24, 24, 45
Amenhotep IV 14, 15, 45
Ammenemes II 13
Amun (god) 7, 12, 13, 15, 16, 25, 37,
    41, 42, 44
Anubis (god) 6, 36, 37
Aten (god) 15, 45

Beni Hasan 13, 20
Book of the Dead 6, 12, 34
burial 40–1

children 17, 26
Cleopatra 5, 25, 45

Deir el-Bahri 7, 13, 14
Deir el-Medina 23, 37
Djoser, King 10, 44

El-Amarna 14, 15, 45
embalming 37, 39
entertainment 32–3

farming 8, 30
food and drink 28–9

Geb (god) 37
Giza 4, 10, 18, 44

hair 11, 26, 27
Hapi (god) 43
Hathor (god) 9, 39
Hatshepsut, Queen 7, 14, 45
hieroglyphs 30, 33, 34–5

Hittites 20, 45
Horus (god) 7, 16, 26, 37, 38
houses 27
hunting and fishing 29
Hyksos 14, 21, 44, 45

invaders 13, 14, 20, 24, 44
Isis (god) 26, 36, 37, 40

Julius Caesar 25

Karnak, temple 7, 13, 42, 44
Khufu, King 18, 19, 44

Libya, Libyans 11, 20, 21

maat 6, 36
Mark Antony 25, 45
mastaba 11, 18
Menes, King 9, 10, 44
Mentuhotep II 12, 13, 44
mummies 5, 37, 38–9
mythology 36–7

Narmer, King 9, 10, 44
Nefertiti, Queen 14
Nephthys (god) 36, 40, 41
Nile, River 4, 8, 13, 21, 28
nomarchs 10, 11, 12, 44
Nubia, Nubians 11, 14, 20, 21
Nun (chaos) 36, 37
Nut (god) 37

Osiris (god) 12, 36–40

papyrus 34, 42

Pharos lighthouse 24, 45
priests 15, 42–3
Ptolemy XII 25
pyramids 4, 5, 10, 18, 44

Rahotep, Prince 11
Rameses II 20, 42, 43, 45
Rameses III 21, 45
Rameses IV 24
Re (god) 12, 15, 16, 36, 37, 39, 41,
    44
religion 36–7, 42–3
Roman Empire, Romans 25, 45

Saqqara 10, 11, 19, 28, 44
scribes 34–5
Sekhmet (god) 37
Seth (god) 16, 37
Seti I 7, 20, 22, 39
Sphinx 5

Thebes 12, 13, 15, 22, 31
Theodosius 25, 45
Thoth (god) 6, 12, 36, 37
toys 27, 33
Tutankhamen, King 15, 17, 20, 23,
    33, 38, 41, 45
Tuthmose II 7, 14, 45
Tuthmose IV 41

Valley of the Kings 16, 22–3, 39, 41
viziers 10, 32

women 17, 26
work 30–1
writing 34–5

Titles in the *History in Art* series include:

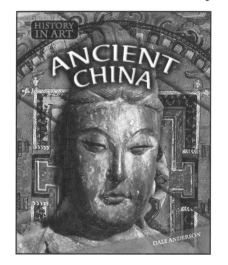

Hardback   1 844 43369 2

Hardback   1 844 43361 7

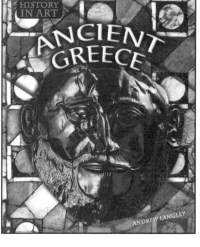

Hardback   1 844 43359 5

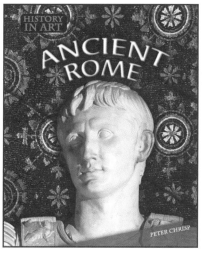

Hardback   1 844 43360 9

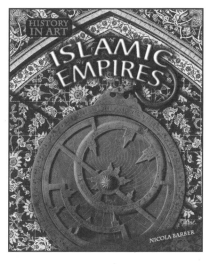

Hardback   1 844 43362 5

Hardback   1 844 43370 6

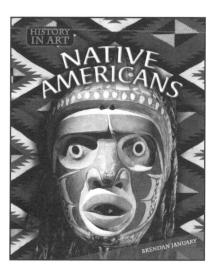

Hardback   1 844 43371 4

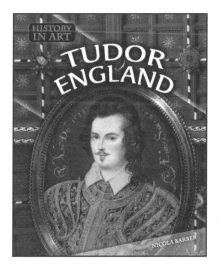

Hardback   1 844 43372 2

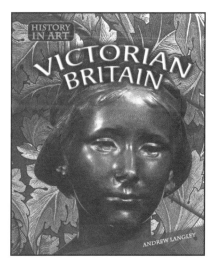

Hardback   1 844 43373 0

Find out about the other titles in this series on our website www.raintreepublishers.co.uk